WHERE TO FIND THE OTHER MONEY

26 Simple Ways Of Earning Extra Income

Contents

If you've been searching for what you can do to help you earn that extra coin, this booklet is a must-read

"Never depend on a single income, make an investment to create a second source"

Warren Buffet

Chapter One

How You Leak Money – 18 Most Common Ways

Before going through the 26 simple ways of earning extra income, first, let me take you through 18 most common ways through which you leak money. Sealing these leaks is vital towards enabling you put your hard earned money into rightful use.

1. **Impulse buying**

   You just walk into say a supermarket, and start purchasing items simply because its payday and you have money in abundance. When you reach home, you realize you've purchased more of items you don't need than those you are in dire need of. And what's the disclaimer on that purchase receipt? *"Goods once sold cannot be returned or exchanged"*!

2. **Purchasing more goods or services outside your budgetary allocation**

   Also commonly referred to as excessive spending, this is one of the top leading causes of money leak! And on a lighter note, you should note that even governments are run on budgets.

3. **Spending simply to please others**

I prefer terming this as unsolicited philanthropy. It may also take the form of spending out of peer influence. You decide to spend your hard earned money on unworthy items or services just to make you not fall out of place with your peers.

4. **Spending beyond your means**

Your mode of transport, where you live and what you eat should always be in alignment with your income, if you yearn to live a financially stress-free life.

5. **Emotional-driven spending**

Spending out of rage, past disappointment, or simply to prove someone wrong. In most cases, this pushes the affected persons into buying more of liabilities than assets.

6. **Spending on wrong investments**

Those that are hurriedly done without the input of trained or experienced investment professionals; they always backfire and eventually make you waste a lot of money!

7. **The 'mentor influence'**

Spending on goods and services that your 'mentor' or someone you look up to may be in possession of i.e. a new trendy cloth or a sleek car (without giving due consideration to your purchasing power). You then rush to borrow money, and after a few months, that item becomes out of fashion. You again shop for the next trendy item in the market? Such will always make you leak endless amounts of money.

8. Delegating your spending responsibility

You send other people to purchase for you goods and services though you have time and even means of transport to realize this. You then end up paying unclear prices and also pay the person you have sent with monetary or non monetary rewards.

9. Abusing debit and credit cards

Withdrawing small sums of cash at the automated teller machines (ATMs) on a regular basis; you'll always end up paying more on associated withdrawal charges. Equally, withdrawing money at alternative money providers charging higher service rates exposes you to paying more charges at the end of the day. Equally, exhausting the limit on your credit card makes you pay higher interest charges, hence leaking your money.

10. Speed spending

Many people, largely men, always spend their money in a hurry, without giving due regard to value or the true price of the items or services they are purchasing. They eventually end up buying items or getting services of lower quality and at inflated prices.

11. Paying bribe

Hiding in the name of 'a thank you tip', to secure services you deserve. Well, to offer a tip is human, but to offer a 'tip' with a left hand whilst expecting your 'purchase' with a right hand is an outright abuse of that 'tip'. And it's worse if the 'tip' involved is money.

12. The 'gift curse'

Unending urge to give out your hard earned valuable assets freely as gifts, even unto people who will never appreciate your effort.

13. Over celebration

This could be due to some great achievement, but organized and done beyond your means of income.

14. Spending on avoidable emergencies

Spending on sudden natural and or un-natural emergencies which may sometimes be within one's control, i.e. sudden loss of job or sickness. One ought to be prepared for such rainy days by taking relevant investment or insurance covers. Equally, set up an emergency kitty where you can conveniently access money for such emergencies.

15. **Abusing phone credit**

The emergence of smart phones has give rise to endless mobile phone applications which heavily rely on internet to function. To access popular social sites such as twitter, Facebook, Whatsapp, Instagram etc via these smart phones, you must have a functioning internet connection. But instead of purchasing internet bundles, or connecting to some free Wifi hotspot, most people rely on their phone's airtime; which is expensive in the long run. Also, continuous borrowing of phone credit makes you incur extra expenses, especially if the credit is given at a fee.

16. **Those little things you don't take serious in the house**

Non use of energy saving bulbs, non switching of electric gadgets not in use, not knowing basic prices of items, leaving money in the pockets of dirty clothes you are giving out for washing etc. These and many others are notorious avenues for money leaks.

17. **Late payment of loans**

Generally, late payment of credit facilities usually attract penalties from associated lenders and creditors in the form of increased interest payment on borrowed loans.

The more late you delay to pay the facility, the more interest you'll end up paying.

18. **Opting to pay interest on a borrowed loan for a longer duration of time, instead of paying part of the principal, or even all of it**

Whether the loan amount is small or big, opting to pay just the interest and not the full amount, or part of it is always an expensive undertaking in the long run. You'll definitely pay more interest on that facility.

Chapter Two

Twenty Six Simple Ways Of Earning Extra Income

Here below are the twenty six simple ways you can consider putting into use to help you earn some extra income:

1. **Take and sell photos online**

   Websites such as iStock, Fotolia, Shutterstock, and Photoshelter allows anyone with a great photo to earn some income by selling it via their platforms.

   If you have a smartphone with good photo feature, or any camera capable of taking great photos, then you can use such sites to earn some extra coins from the photos you take.

2. **Hire out your car, boat, motorbike or bicycle**

   If you have any of these, you can hire them out to close friends, family or neighbours at a fee.

   You can also link up with Taxi service providers such as Uber and use their platform to access clients, or to offer your driver-services (if you qualify).

3. **Do you have a skill you can trade for $5?**

If your answer is yes then head to Fiverr.com , create a profile and offer it. Fiverr.com offers a virtual marketplace where people sell and buy services from as low as $5.

Are you a graphic designer? Can you edit documents? Can you produce short videos or audios? Can you write or review articles? Can you review books, songs or products? You have all these options and many more available at Fiverr.com. The beauty of using this platform is that you can complete a number offers in a couple of minutes and move on to others. And it's what you can do and the time you are willing to put into it which determines how much you take home at the end of the day.

4. **Run errands for other people**

If you have means of transport, you can run errands for other people. Your friends, colleagues, or neighbors may be looking for someone to help them move to a new house/home, or to assist them pick up some items from the local store. Watch out for such opportunities and grab them. You can also advertise your services on social media platforms such as local Facebook groups and through Thumbtack.

5. **Create and monetize a blog or website**

Are you an expert in a certain field or subject? Do you have a unique story or experience that you would love to share with others? Create a blog or a website and monetize it (put Google Ads or Google affiliate ads such as Infolinks or Chitika adds on that blog or website to earn you some extra income). A number of people have ended up quitting their well-paying jobs to concentrate on building their blogs or websites due to massive income they generate from ads placed on those sites. Don't you think it's a cool way to boost your income?

6. **Charge some fee to take professional photos or play music at weddings or events**

If you have the experience of taking professional photos, you can consider charging some fee to do so. If you can also play music instruments such as a violin or have DJ skills, you can also consider advertising your skills for consideration at events. You can use social platforms or sites such as Craigslist, Thumbtack., gigmasters.com, weddingwire.com, and gigsalad.com to advertise your skills.

7. **Take up mystery shopping assignments**

If you can spare some time, then you can consider picking up a mystery shopping gig, and provide feedback to the provider. To access scam-free mystery shopping tasks, visit Mystery Shopping Providers Association.

8. **Sell items you don't use**

You can assemble items you no longer use at home or those that you don't find good use of and sell them on Sell and Buy platforms such as *Olx, local Facebook Sell or Buy Groups, Craigslist, EBay* etc. You can sell those old electronics, used text books, oversized or undersized clothes and many more.

The maximum amount of money you can raise from doing this depends on the value and quantity of the items you are selling, and the effort you'll be willing to put towards realizing success.

9. **Find avenues of earning more income from your current job**

If you are in a commission based job, then this is the time to work extra hard, or extra smart and earn more commissions through available channels. And if there is an opportunity for overtime payment, then you should utilize it towards earning more.

10. **Find a better paying job:**

If the nature of your job is kind of fixed on a certain salary scale, then you can consider looking for a secondary job or a part time job elsewhere (as long as it doesn't conflict with your current job), to help you boost your income. This might sound unconventional, but truth is, you are not going to work all your life. If you believe you are not being paid according to the kind of work you do and the value you bring to that organization, then you should consider looking for a better paying job elsewhere. This would not only boost your current income, but also your lifetime earnings. And in case your employer might be unwilling to let you go, then you can consider negotiating for a pay rise.

11. Lower your expenses

Reducing your expenses doesn't mean that you are now resorting to living a cheap life. It means cutting back on those excesses. It means lowering your wastage. If you eat out often, then this is the time to make adjustments and start eating at home or carry packed food to your work place. That TV subscription you rarely use, or that monthly membership subscription to a yoga class you rarely attend can take a back seat for a while .Find what to cut back on to help you save some money.

12. Can you spare some time to take surveys and read mails?

Many websites offer platforms where you are paid to take certain short surveys, listen to certain songs for a short duration of time, or read some short-worded emails. A good example is Inbox Dollars. You'll join for free and you get $5 just for signing up. And once your earnings reach stipulated amount, then you can withdraw your earnings through requesting for a check or receive it through your PayPal account. And once you sign up with them, you'll continue getting other unending offers from other websites linked to them. You can also check SwagBucks.

13. Become a translator

If you are gifted with a spare language (bilingual or multilingual), you can consider doing part time translation work. Check Translatorstown, Peopleperhour, iWriter, Freelancer, Gengo, UpWork or Guru if you can find some translation assignment. You can also advertise your services on social media sites to help access more clients.

14. Find some freelancing work

If you have problem solving skills, or you are a people person, you can consider pursuing customer service or virtual assistant freelancing work on sites such as *Craigslist,* VirtualAssistants.com, Fiverr, Freelancer, UpWork, Guru and even on Zirtual.

And if you can write academic or business articles, you can pick up assignments on iWriter, Peopleperhour, Freelancer, UpWork or Guru. Depending on your skill and effort, Freelancing offers opportunities for unlimited rewards. If you are skilled in design work, you can bid for jobs at sites such as 99Designs.com.

15. Don't ignore those sweepstakes and opportunities to enter raffle draws

As proverbially connoted, you never know what you can achieve until you try. But do this responsibly. Don't insist on stopping only if you win the jackpot. Know when to pause, and when to eventually stop.

16. Can you spare your home or some room within your home/house

Many people make good money by renting out their homes or a room within their homes to tourists or travelers. You can access potential clients through sites such as vrbo.com, Expedia.com, airbnb.com, Jumuia travel, booking.com, roomorama.com, and Trip Advisor.

17. Take up a tutor job

Are you skilled in a particular subject or topic? You can charge a fee to tutor students or even adults within your locality. You can also find tutor related assignments on sites such as Chegg Tutors, and Tutor.com. Equally, you can also consider teaching online courses via sites such as as Chegg Tutors teach.udemy.com, studypool.com, or Skillshare.

18. Raise money through crowd funding

There are several crowd funding platforms you can utilize to raise money towards funding your dream ideas, or for any other cause. Kickstarter, Indiegogo, GoFundMe, Crowdfunder, Crowdsupply and YouCaring are just a few examples of such sites. The trick in raising money through Crowd funding is to write a compelling message that would lure people to donate towards your cause.

19. Join a focus group

Focus group platforms such as focusgroup.com, mysurvey.com,harrispollonline.com,focuspointeglobal.com, ipoll.com, inspiredopinions.com and swagbucks.com lists available opportunities in select areas, and equally pays you to complete certain surveys. Typically, focus groups rely on select participants to solicit for feedback on products and services offered by various brands, organizations, and businesses. This is vital in market research for the involved entities.

20. Sit or walk pets

You can do this on part time or full time engagement. You can equally consider taking daytime or night time offers. Notably, you can find offers on platforms such as *Craigslist,* Care.com, and dogvacay.com.

21. Coach others at a fee

Do you have an experience or skill in Yoga? Can you mentor others in areas such as public speaking? Are you experienced in advanced computer packages such as Excel, Spss or Stata? Can you train others on how to skate or how to play any game? Then find interested parties and coach them at a fee. You can create a website or advertise your services through social media sites.

22. Make money from your craft

Can you make those unique handmade items? Can you make jewelry, or knit unique items? Can you draw or curve portraits? What unique craft do you have that you can sell to others? Use websites such as etsy.com or craftcoxes.com to access clients and sell such crafts.

23. Be an independent tour guide

Can you devote some time to give tourists or travelers and in-depth tour guide around your locality, town, city or country? You can market your services on social media platforms and on websites such as vayable.com.

24. Buy select items at wholesale prices (discounted prices) and sell them for profit

You can buy toys at wholesale prices and sell them at kids' events. Equally, you can buy bottled water at wholesale prices and sell them at events such as a friend's wedding or at local parties. Just find any item which has proven selling potential, get it at wholesale price (discounted price) and then sell it at a profitable retail price.

25. Earn from Media ads

Is your home close to main road or highway? You can rent a space on the wall of your house for an erection of a media billboard at a cost. Equally, you can allow ads to be placed on your car at a cost. Check examples at freecarmedia.com. If you feel you look gorgeous, you can consider modeling on part time or full time basis.

26. **Can you risk being a guinea pig?**

Can you risk being used in a clinical trial in exchange for some good amount of money? Then you can check for available offers from sites such as clinicaltrials.gov

N/B: Some of the suggested ways might not offer you the *get-it-quick* or so much money, but at least, they offer you avenues of making extra money in a more relaxed and fun way.

Chapter Three

13 Financially Healthy And Highly Rewarding Habits To Exercise

One
Live Within Your Income

"Never depend on single income. Make investment to create a second source"

Warren Buffett

You were never born to merely exist and pay unending bills and debts. There is a lot of financial abundance in the world which you too, have a right to tap into and live a financially fulfilling life, just like many other people.

However, you must first note that no amount of money will ever be enough to fully satisfy your day to day financial needs. Consequently, taking endless loans in pursuit of meeting your daily financial needs is a gamble you'll seldom win! In the end, you'll simply get highly indebted and will never have peace of mind!

You must learn to slow down on spending money you don't have and start running your befitting financial race. Live the life you can afford, within your income. Stay away from the temptation of borrowing money to spend on items you can comfortably purchase from your own income or savings.

Before you hurriedly embark on spending your hard-earned money on any item, here below are the **four vital questions you must ask yourself to help cushion you against unnecessary or excessive spending**.

The four vital questions you must ask yourself before spending money on any item

Question number one
Is it necessary? - Can your life go on smoothly without purchasing that item or service?

Question number two
How urgent do I need it? - What's the level of urgency involved? In other words, how bad do you want it?

Question number three

Can I afford it? - In other words, can you comfortably acquire it without necessarily resorting to borrowing money elsewhere?

Question number four

Will I be getting value for my money? - Is it original or counterfeit? How long is it expected to last? And is there any other seller offering a similar item at a lesser cost?

If it's necessary, it's urgent, you can afford it without borrowing money elsewhere, and you are getting value for your money, then that's a green light to purchase that given item or service. But if you can't confidently answer all or at least three of the above questions, then that's a red light on that spending.

Always be contended with the things you can comfortably afford. Enjoy them and work hard towards increasing your income to enable you afford more. Your way of life should be a true reflection of your real income. Don't fake it or live a seemingly richer life that you can't comfortably sustain. Living within your income will help you thwart the urge of being lured into any avoidable debt.

Two
Create A Secondary Source of Income

"Don't tell me what you value, show me your budget, and I'll tell you what you value" Joe Biden

The day you realize that no amount of money is enough is the day you finally graduate into adulthood. No amount of money is ever sufficient to completely quench the unending thirst of human financial needs.

We all want more. We all desire to be in possession of the beautiful things this life can offer, yet these things are largely accessed financially.

The moment you establish your first source of income, finding a secondary source of income should be a priority. Even in the Bible, God established four rivers to water the blessed Garden of Eden. Why wouldn't He allow just one river to water Eden? Wasn't it a blessed garden?

You will always thrive in abundance when you rely on more than once source of income. And after securing the secondary source of income, work on the third, the fourth, the fifth, the sixth,.......sources of income.

Have diverse sources of income. Never depend on one tributary, it might dry up sooner than you think and expose your world to drought!

Three
Budget For Every Coin You Earn

Except for emergencies, always budget for what you spend your money on. I'm sure you've heard more than a thousand times the need of having a budget for every coin you earn. Why don't you commit putting this into action?

Living without a budget is like trusting a toddler to successfully crawl across a busy highway. It's that risky!

Budgeting will help you keep track of your earnings vs. expenditure, and enable you put a right cap on your spending excesses.

With budgeting, you'll stop viewing luxury living as some wish in a dreamland since you will always find slots for your personal enjoyments, allowing you to gratify yourself as you go on with life.

Having a right budget in place will always offer you a perfect escape route towards living a truly financially healthy lifestyle.

"Rule No. 1: Never lose money. Rule No. 2: Never forget rule No.1"
Warren Buffett

Four
Save and Invest

It's never how much you have, how much you earn, or how early or how late you receive your wages which determine your level of financial success. It's how you put into use that which you earn.

Truth is, you are not going to work forever. Someday, you will be forced to leave the comfort of that business, or that office through old age, retirement, termination, resignation, or even on medical grounds (God forbid!) etc. You must therefore, learn to put your financial house in order before that bleak day arrives.

To live a financially secure and healthy life, you must save and invest part of your earnings, that windfall, or that bonus. An age old proven savings principle is to save 10% of your net earnings, for a specific period of time, say five or ten years. Afterwards, you should carefully invest that saved amount somewhere safe where it will earn you some interest.

When you invest money, you put it to work for you. As a result, it should be able to earn you some income at the end of the period. Significantly, you'll need to invest the money somewhere secure where you can access it whenever you desire to.

If you save and invest part of your earnings wisely, you shall have provided in advance for your future financial needs and those of your family. And even in your absence, the continuity of your family shall have been guaranteed, financially.

To dig a little deep on savings and investments, let me take you through some of **the most common terms used in the savings and investment world.**

- ✓ **Savings**: An amount of money kept aside, mostly in a financial institution such as a bank, for future use. Or an amount of money not spent on current expenditures.

- ✓ **Income**: What you earn from your investment. Examples of income include coupons obtained from mature bonds, dividends payments from unit trusts/shares held, and interest earned from a fixed deposit account.

- ✓ **Risk**: Generally, risk is defined as a situation involving exposure to certain danger. All investments have certain elements of risk that an investor has to bear. Notably, there is an age-old financial maxim that *the greater the risk, the higher the projected rewards.* However, when investing your hard-earned money, you should keenly understand the risks involved in order to make an effective decision on whether to commit your money or not.

- ✓ **Investment horizon:** This is the amount of time you take to invest in order to realize your financial objectives.

- ✓ **Return on investment**: This is the gross gain or gross loss that you realize out of an investment. If say you invested in an item, then the return on that investment can either be a gain or loss in value of that item.

- ✓ **Net returns:** The total returns from your investment less operational, administrative, and other related costs. It's the actual profit or loss after eliminating accompanying costs.

- ✓ **Capital gain/loss**: Simply the gain or loss that you make as a result of selling an asset or product at a price above or below the price you paid to acquire it.

Factors you should consider before saving or investing any amount of money

Below are some of the most vital factors to consider when faced with an investment option to settle on.

- ✓ **First, identify your investment goals with clarity**

  What do you specifically want to achieve by saving or investing that money? Do you want it to grow, or do you just want it to be kept safe regardless of any expected profit? And how long are you willing to wait for it to mature?

- ✓ **Do you have an emergency fund?**

  Before committing any amount of money towards savings or investment, ensure you have a cash reserve or a source of income capable of sustaining you throughout the investment period.

- ✓ **Understand the risks involved**

  Are you capable of bearing the risks linked to your savings or investment? Are you able to move on in case you unfortunately lose all, or part of that money?

Deciding to invest part or all of your money has accompanying rewards: negatives and positives. Are you able to live with the consequences of your decision to invest that money?

✓ **Carry out an in-depth research on other various savings and investment options available**

Don't settle on any savings or investment option with minimal rewards when the most rewarding and most secure option is just a few minutes/hours/days of research away. Visit local financial institutions and insurance companies to explore various products that have the potential to offer you better returns on your investment.

✓ **Read in between the lines**

Go through the terms and conditions of the option you desire to settle on to establish what is on offer. Know what you'll gain by holding on to your investment till maturity, and what you may lose in case you abruptly withdraw part of or the entire amount. You will always have a peace of mind by investing in a product you have full knowledge of.

✓ **Establish the cost of your investment**

One true yet sad fact with most investment products from a number of financial institutions is that they have certain hidden costs. Most clients only get to know about those hidden charges at the maturity of the invested amount, or when withdrawing the invested amount. Nonetheless, such costs (if any), are usually minimal and should not bar you from realizing your larger investment goals. It's therefore beneficial to always invest from a point of knowledge.

✓ **Have plan B**

What do you do when your sole investment option fails to live to your expectation? Do you just walk away heart-broken, vowing never to invest any money again? Investments aren't matters of life and death. You may fail in one but succeed in another. The best investment strategy is to always find ways of spreading or minimizing risks associated with your investment. If you have adequate cash, it's advisable to diversify your investments.

Below are some of the today's secure **savings and investments options you can consider**

❖ **Buying shares in the stock market**

Shares are generally issued by companies in bid to raise capital from investors. The moment you buy any company's share, you become its shareholder and is rightfully entitled to the company's share of any dividends it declares and pays out. Across the globe, people buy shares in hope that their prices will someday increase. Others buy them in pursuit of dividend payments, or as a shield against inflation.

Notably, companies listed in various stock exchange markets pay dividends out of profits they make (if any). In certain instances, a listed company may decide to re-invest its profits into the business. And in the event the company is faced with liquidation but you still own part of its shares, then you are rightfully entitled to its remaining assets; but only after all its creditors have been settled.

When you own any company's shares, you have an option of selling them the moment the share price increases in value, or hold on to the shares when prices are low or unfavorable.

Investing in shares is ideal for economic-savvy persons, people who can forecast the future performances or behaviors of listed companies. However, with good advice from trustworthy stockbrokers or investment advisers, you can take a stab at buying any advised listed companies' shares.

Remember, *'you lose 100% of chances you fail to take.'* Most people are afraid of investing their money in the stock market. This has give room to a smaller portion of the population who are currently reaping heavy returns from various stock markets across the globe.

❖ **Open a fixed deposit account**

This is another exciting option offered by several financial institutions. They allow you to deposit or invest a specific amount of money at an agreed interest rate, for a specific duration of time.

This option is evidently better than merely opening a savings account since it has better returns on savings. However, you will be required to deposit your money for a specific period of time, without withdrawing any portion of it. In return, your money will yield some favorable interest payable at the end of an agreed period.

You can consider putting your money in a fixed deposit account if you have no urgent/immediate use of it. And before putting your cash in any fixed deposit account, carefully go through the offer from the financial institution giving you the service, and ensure you properly understand the pros and cons of keeping your money with them. It's also advisable to compare other offers from different financial institutions to enable you get the best deal for your money.

❖ **Invest in a structured deposit**

A structured deposit has an investment option. It's different from a fixed deposit account since it offers potential for higher returns. But on the other hand, it has higher risks; such as receiving lower amounts than your expectation. The returns on structured deposits depend on the performance of assets/products which the money are invested in. Such may include shares, bonds, and other fixed income securities etc.

You will receive the principal amount you have invested in a structured deposit as long as you do not withdraw the money before maturity. If you leave it to maturity, you will be paid the principal amount and the agreed interest; provided the financial institution does not negate on the deal. Therefore, the credit risk of the financial institution holding your deposit is significant in helping you gauge the quality of your returns.

❖ **Invest in bonds**

A bond is form of borrowing. It's a debt security issued by a borrower i.e. a government or a company seeking to raise funds from the financial stock market(s).

A bond is classified as a fixed income security; it pays a steady flow of income at intervals throughout its life. Bonds are largely offered for a period of more than ten years (though there are certain instances where some may be offered for periods less than ten years).

Other fixed income securities are Bills (debt securities maturing in less than one year), and Notes (debt securities maturing between one to ten years).

The life or duration of a bond is referred to as its tenure, and the interest from bonds are known as coupons. The rates of coupons are expressed as a percentage of the principal amounts, known as face values or par values. The prices of bonds are expressed as a % of the face value. Once a bond matures, it is redeemed at a face value, and those who hold the bonds are generally paid one hundred percent of the face value.

There are certain bonds which do not offer coupon payments at all. They are known as zero-coupon bonds. The prices of zero-coupon bonds are mostly discounted at the bonds' par values. i.e., a zero-coupon bond of say $10,000 par value is issued for 10 years at $7000. It means that you will be paying $7000 for a bond which will be worth $10,000 in ten years.

The prices of bonds are usually quoted as a percentage of the par value i.e. a bond of 110% or a bond of 80%.

Before investing in any bond, first, carefully go through its terms and conditions. Read in between the lines and clearly understand the offer. As a general precaution, never invest money you intend to use on emergencies. Ensure you have adequate financial liquidity to sustain you as you wait for the bond to mature. And most significant, keenly analyze the expected performance of the bond during its tenure. You should involve services of a trusted financial advisor, or you can as well carry out the analysis on your own - if you have the relevant know-how.

It's the credit quality of the issuer of a bond which determines the quality of the bond's yield. Mostly, bonds of higher qualities are issued by governments. Equally, companies or institutions linked to governments such as banks also do offer quality bonds. When investing in bonds offered by corporate entities, go for those issued by good-rated corporates.

❖ **Invest in unit trusts**

A unit trust or unit fund is another favorable investment option offered by banks, investment banks, other financial institutions, and insurance companies. Your money is pooled together with other investors', and thereafter, carefully invested in a portfolio of assets according to the fund's declared investment goals and best fitting investment approaches. In a nutshell, unit trusts are generally managed by experienced fund managers, and do operate on a trust structure.

The price of each unit correlates to the fund's net asset value. It's determined by dividing the current market value of the fund's net assets by the number of outstanding units. Your main gain from investing in unit trusts is realized when the prices of the units rises above the initial price you paid. And notably, a good number of unit trusts do pay dividends at certain stipulated times.

The beauty of investing in unit trusts is that it gives you a safer avenue for investing in a diversified range of assets, thus minimizing your risk exposure. It also grants you a secure access to markets or assets which may be more costly if you were to purchase them on your own. If you love to own shares in the stock market, but lack the necessary know-how, you can test out with investing in unit trusts.

And most significant, unit trusts offer you flexible options to choose from. If you want total safety for your invested money, you may settle on unit trusts with capital preservation and income generation. Here, it is the investment banks or insurance companies who bear the risk associated with investing your money. But if you long for more appreciation of your money and you are willing to accept greater risks, then you can settle on funds inclined towards helping your invested money grow.

❖ **Re-invest in your business**

When you feel satisfied with the returns from your business, the least you can do is to plough back all, or part of profits gained into the business. By doing so, you are positioning the business for more yield. Equally, you can re-invest in the business with the focus of expanding its operations.

❖ **Be an angel investor**

Do you have a keen eye for identifying those startups with possibly good future potential growth and returns? Today, there are endless startups in pursuit of either financial or technical support. You can carefully identify one, invest in it and reap the sweet rewards later after it has stabilized.

"Beware the investment activity that produces applause; the great moves are usually greeted by yawns"
Warren Buffet

Five
Avoid Crowd-Guided Savings And Investment Approaches

You must safeguard your savings and investments from avoidable potential losses.

Why would you sacrifice part of your earnings for all those five, ten or twenty years, only to end up losing them in an avoidable unscrupulous deal?

Today, there is a heap of wrong financial advice given by 'financial experts' whose education backgrounds and experiences lie in other fields. Truth is, most financial and investment institutions today are more profit driven. Instead of giving their clients value for money, they are solely focused on remaining profitable.

You must therefore learn to listen to your instinct as you seek for any savings or investment related advice.

That everyone in your office is excited at investing in certain shares should not be an excuse for you to hurriedly invest in those shares as well without any sound financial or investment advice.

"Can anything be so elegant as to have few wants, and to serve them one's self?"
Ralph Waldo Emerson

Six
Only Get Into Debt You Can Afford

You've endlessly heard that *you should never test the depth of a river with both feet.* Do you think you can have a comfortable sleep, or be able to move around peacefully, knowing that you used your car, house, business, or some precious household item as a collateral to a credit facility you've failed to pay back, with no possible signs of being able to pay up?

Literally, borrowing signifies some form of "incompleteness". It may either turn you into a master - when someone owes you, or a slave - when you owe someone. It's like a two edged sword. You must therefore, discipline yourself to only borrow money you can comfortably repay. Significantly, learn to only get into debt when you're in need of purchasing items with appreciating values, or for any viable business venture.

To purchase assets with non-increasing values, you should save towards acquiring them, or purchase them from your own income. You must learn to manage your appetite for taking loans unnecessarily, as such might trap you into the bottomless pit of debt. Well, debt isn't bad, but unplanned debt is like poison in a nicely prepared meal!

"These days, you've gotta milk a dollar out of every dime."
Gayle Forman, Where She Went

Seven
Spend More on Items Offering You Savings on Purchases

Why would you want to buy a new television set from a high end retailer when your next door neighbor who is relocating to another country is offering you a similar one month old TV for sale at half the original price?

And do you really need to take lunch every day at that high end hotel (with highly priced menu) while you have a fridge and a microwave in the office to help you store and heat up that packed lunch from home?

And why would you want to sleep out in that fancy hotel when your home/house is just a stone throw away?

And strange still, why would you save to purchase a car if you have no urgent use of it? Why would you insist on buying it if you have no adequate money to buy its insurance cover, to fuel it, and or to service it?

"The best time to buy a home is always five years ago"
Ray Brown

Eight
Own Your Dwelling Place

Own where you live. Or any amount of money you pay towards rent should be geared towards owning that apartment or house.

Paying rent is a liability, but if its payment is geared towards owning that house someday, then that's an asset.

Owning your place of dwelling will not only offer you convenience, freedom and peace of mind, but will equally help you free that *rent money* to utilize on other projects such as savings, investments and or on any emergent financial need.

"Fake friends; those who only drill holes under your boat to get it leaking; those who discredit your ambitions and those who pretend they love you, but behind their backs they know they are in to destroy your legacies"

Israelmore Ayivor

Nine

Shun the Company of Negative Financial Influencers

Never be afraid of saying NO to unjustifiable financial solicitations, be it from friends, relatives or colleagues.

A famous connotation goes; *show me your bank account balance and I will show you your friends.* The world has conditioned us to "hang out" with people within our 'classes'. We consequently end up having friends whose earning and spending abilities are almost commensurate with ours.

But there are some friends and colleagues who will always want to take advantage of your financial innocence and exploit you to their advantage. As an example, they will never hesitate taking you out to the best hotel around for lunch, but end up making you pay the bill.

Equally, they will want to lure you to purchase a personal car to take them out every weekend, while they buy homes whose values keep appreciating each month. While you are focused on pimping that car to match their taste, they on the other hand are working on acquiring a secondary house, or even a parcel of land somewhere.

"Hang out" with people who respect your wallet. Not those crafty scavengers who retire to bed while scheming on how to extract money from you the next day.

Avoid those stingy, night-club-thirsty brokes who can't even buy for themselves drinking water at that fancy club they frequent courtesy of your wallet.

Always remember that there are friends who will only stick by your side all is rosy, but you'll never see them during your financially trying times.

"Neither a borrower nor a lender be, for loan oft loses both itself and friend, and borrowing dulls the edge of husbandry"
William Shakespeare

Ten

Never Lend Money You Can't Afford to Live Without

Lending money to very close friends or relatives, especially to people who can easily take advantage of your generosity usually have ugly endings.

It's never easy as an individual to successfully recover money which has fallen in the hands of *a wrong borrower*. It's therefore, essential to arm yourself with the below **six simple safety measures you can adopt to help you lend your money safely**, if you must. Here they are:

✓ **Only lend money you are willing to lose**

> If you are not willing to lose that money, don't lend it to anyone. If you can't live without it, don't give it out. It's that simple!

✓ **Establish the credit rating/credit score of the borrower**

> Technically, most individual lenders would want to shy away from taking this route, but in case you want to guarantee the safety of your money, you should ask the lender to provide you with his or her credit rating/score, obtained from a reputational credit reference provider. This will help you establish any

history of unpaid or defaulted payments by the borrower.

✓ **Know the personal details of the borrower**

Know where the borrower lives, workplace, permanent home address, some close relatives, friends, and even family members you can contact in case of default, or in case the borrow is unreachable.

✓ **Ask for guarantee and, or a guarantor**

You can ask the borrower to provide collateral of a similar or more value for the borrowed amount, or have a reputable individual act as a guarantor to the borrower. In case of any trouble in payment, or total default in payment, you'll know where to turn to.

✓ **Keep an updated track of the borrower**

You can occasionally call the borrower just to get to know how he/she is fairing on. You can equally occasionally call the guarantor, if any, to ascertain the wellbeing of the borrower.

✓ **And why not insure that money?**

Practically, this might not be possible in several countries due to unavailability of relevant insurance covers. Designing appropriate insurance covers for individual money lenders is literally an underwriting headache to many insurance providers. But if you come across a relevant insurance cover which can shield you against losing money you are lending, simply grab it.

"Into each life some rain must fall/Some days must be dark and dreary"
Henry Wadsworth Longfellow

Eleven
Have An Emergency Kitty

An emergency kitty will always shield you from viewing credit as your safety net. And in the event of exposure to unavoidable life's emergencies or tragedies such as sickness, job loss, or even death, you'll always have somewhere to turn to for financial help.

"To keep the body in good health is a duty... otherwise we shall not be able to keep our mind strong and clear"
Buddha

Twelve
Take Good Care of Your Health

Most probably, you've heard that your health is your wealth.

Go for those periodical checkups, eat healthy foods, stay on diet, drink lots of water, meditate often, and do regular exercises.

Do whatever you can to stay healthy. And whatever strategies you adopt to help you acquire more money, ensure your health is never compromised. After all, what would be the essence of acquiring all that wealth only to lose your life suddenly on avoidable health-related grounds?

"I believe that we all have a responsibility to give back. No one becomes successful without lots of hard work, support from others, and a little luck. Giving back creates a virtuous cycle that makes everyone more successful"

Ron Conway

Thirteen
Learn to Give Back

You will never lack by giving. As a sign of gratitude, always give something to those less fortunate members of the society. Give to those who may never be in any position to pay you back.

What special talent do you have? Can you find some time to mentor others? Use that unique gift you have to lift up or encourage someone else. The biggest secret to being alive is in giving back. Give freely, as much as you possibly can.

"The secret to wealth is simple: Find a way to do more for others than anyone else does. Become more valuable. Do more. Give more. Be more. Serve more."

Tony Robbins